Essential Question
Why do people run for public office?

The Wolves of Yellowstone

by
Kathy White

illustrated by
Bryan Berry

CHAPTER 1

A Sad Day in Yellowstone

A long and eerie howl echoed across the canyon. The wolves in Yellowstone National Park instantly knew that Gray Tail, the leader of the Wolf Council, was dead.

Silver Fire shook her head sadly. "Gray Tail was a wise, kind, and strong leader. He was always willing to go the extra mile for us."

Moondance sighed as he watched their pups, Little Smudge and White Feet, tumbling and growling in the autumn leaves. He smiled softly and said, "Gray Tail tolerated the younger pups yipping and pouncing on him, even when they pulled his raggedy old ears."

Silver Fire laughed. "And no matter how weary he was or how silly my questions might have seemed, Gray Tail always listened."

"I guess that's why he was a great leader," Moondance said, sighing again. "What will we do without Gray Tail? Who will lead the Wolf Council?"

Silver Fire had been wondering the same thing. She tilted her head as she thought. "There's Bright Star—she's a great hunter and very intelligent."

"She's also very young," Moondance said. "She doesn't have enough experience to lead the Wolf Council."

"Well, if you want a bold wolf, there's always Black Streak of Mollie's pack."

Moondance snarled and narrowed his eyes. "He's dangerous. He might be strong and bold, but he's not wise."

Little Smudge whimpered, "He's scary. He said he could eat me. I might be small, but I'm as fast as an arrow."

"I know," Silver Fire said as she gently nuzzled Little Smudge.

The Yellowstone wolves would have to choose a new leader soon. The four wolf packs were getting ready to separate into different areas of the park for winter. The new leader must be chosen from one of the packs before then, but Silver Fire couldn't think of anyone who was good enough to replace Gray Tail.

CHAPTER 2
Black Streak Breaks the Rules

The next morning, Silver Fire led her pack to a place where she had hidden some elk meat. Black Frost wasn't hungry. He paced anxiously and then lay down.

Silver Fire stopped chewing. "Are you feeling sick?" she asked.

Black Frost shook his head, but he looked worried. "Black Streak took food from a human yesterday, so the rangers have closed the area until they find the wolf responsible. What if they blame me?"

Everyone stopped eating. Black Streak was a troublemaker, and Black Frost looked just like him. Black Frost was tall and lanky with a black lightning-shaped mark in his fur.

Silver Fire thought about one of the most important rules among the wolves in Yellowstone: Wild animals must never approach people. Animals that broke this rule could be removed from the park by rangers.

Silver Fire stood up. "I'm going to look for Black Streak. He needs to follow the rules."

The others told her not to get involved, but Silver Fire was determined. She needed to find Black Streak before the rangers found him.

Silver Fire ran swiftly toward the ridge on the eastern side of the lake, where his scent was strongest. Then she made her way down through the pine trees. She stopped and noticed a wolf in the distance trotting toward the boundary of the park. Silver Fire howled, then rushed down the slope toward Black Streak, trying to catch him before he left the park.

"Thank goodness I found you," Silver Fire gasped when she had finally caught up to Black Streak. "You almost stepped outside the Yellowstone boundary."

Black Streak narrowed his eyes. "I know where I am, Silver Fire." He glanced at some cattle and sheep in a nearby pasture. "I've been here many times before."

Silver Fire was shocked. "If you cross the park boundary onto ranchers' land, all of the Yellowstone wolves will be punished."

"There will only be trouble if a wolf with a radio-tracking collar accompanies me," he said, "so you'll have to turn around and go back to your pack. I, on the other hand, can do whatever I like."

"But if someone sees you—" Silver Fire warned.

"They won't," he insisted. "I move like the wind, and I'm as quiet as a mouse."

The sound of a car engine startled them. Black Streak snapped at Silver Fire, "You never saw me here." He sprinted into the trees before the rangers saw him.

Two rangers appeared. "That wolf sure is a long way from home," one of them said. "What do you think she's doing here? She's not the one with the black streak that the ranchers saw crossing the park border."

Silver Fire didn't wait to hear more. She raced back up the hill away from the rangers. Her heart was pounding, but at the same time, she felt stronger and bolder than she had ever felt before.

She had been thinking about the kind of wolf that should replace Gray Tail on the Wolf Council. Now she was sure about what she needed to do.

CHAPTER 3
Silver Fire and the Wolf Council

"I want to lead the Wolf Council," Silver Fire announced at the council meeting the next morning. The wolves stood around her, and her own pack looked on, eyes sparkling with pride.

"You're very young," said Magnus, one of the older wolves. "Why should we trust you to lead us?"

Silver Fire spoke clearly. "My ancestors were all strong leaders. I have many skills, including kindness and teamwork. I'm strong enough to hunt alone, but I want to hunt with my pack. I could break the rules and leave the park or steal food, but I do what is best for the wolves of Yellowstone. Gray Tail taught us that some rules are necessary for survival."

A few wolves in Mollie's pack began to grumble. Black Streak glared at Silver Fire. Silver Fire continued, "The wolves of Yellowstone need to cooperate and share responsibilities."

Black Streak pushed his way to the front. "Wolves have rights and freedoms, too. We're the strongest animals in the park. Why should we stay within the boundaries when there's good food out there?" He pointed past the park boundary.

"Because the rangers will take us away," Silver Fire answered. "Besides," she continued, "we don't need their food. We're proud to be wild animals, not scavengers. That's what Gray Tail would say, and I agree."

Silver Fire looked around at the wolves. "I intend to run for leader of the Wolf Council. Do I have an opponent?"

Black Streak faced her and declared, "I will run against you. I will be a strong leader who is not afraid to make decisions."

Some of the wolves gasped and stepped back. Silver Fire did not react to Black Streak's words but held his stare. Finally, Black Streak looked away.

Magnus announced, "We need time to think about what we really need in a leader. We shall meet tomorrow night to vote."

CHAPTER 4
A New Leader Is Chosen

"Sorry, little ones, you're too young to vote," Silver Fire told Little Smudge and White Feet on their way to the election the next evening. "Your turn will come when you're older," she reassured them.

The three wolves started to cross the road together, but several large wolves from Mollie's pack blocked their path.

"We want to talk to you alone," Scarface hissed at Silver Fire.

Silver Fire turned to her pups. "You two race each other to the council clearing. Your father is already there. Find him and wait for me."

The pups nodded, then tore off through the trees. Silver Fire felt calmer once the two young wolves had gone, but she was still nervous. The Mollie wolves didn't look friendly. She told them, "Make it quick, or I'll be late for the meeting."

"That would be a shame, wouldn't it, boys?" Scarface sneered. The others snorted as if he had told a good joke.

As four of the Mollie wolves started to move toward her, Silver Fire raced across the road in front of a bus taking tourists out of the park. The passengers yelled, "Wolf!" and the driver swung the bus onto the grass.

The bus separated Silver Fire from the Mollies, making it easy for her to escape from them. Soon she saw the council clearing ahead and heard Magnus's voice.

Silver Fire arrived in the clearing and searched for Little Smudge and White Feet. She saw them with Moondance and sighed with relief.

Then another face caught her eye. Black Streak stood scowling next to Magnus. The crowd was so quiet that Silver Fire could hear her own breathing. The sound of winged insects buzzed in her ears.

Magnus called to Silver Fire. His eyes were warm and full of understanding. He said carefully, "Your pups told us that some Mollie wolves stopped you to ask questions." Black Streak's scowl deepened. "I trust that you still want to campaign for leader of the council?" Magnus asked.

Silver Fire nodded. Then she and Black Streak turned away from the other wolves and faced the forest. They were not allowed to see which wolves voted for them.

Magnus announced to the crowd, "You know the rules. You can vote only once, and you must be an adult." Then he said, "Howl long and loud if you vote for Black Streak."

The howls echoed thinly in the cool night air. Mollie's pack was the loudest.

Magnus waited for the sound to fade. Then he said, "Howl long and loud if you vote for Silver Fire."

The wolves sang like a well-rehearsed chorus. It was so loud and overwhelming that Silver Fire's chest vibrated.

"Turn around, please," Magnus said. "Silver Fire, you are our new leader. Gray Tail would be proud to know that you are passing on what he taught."

Silver Fire noticed Black Streak's disappointed face. She whispered to him, "I'll need your help. If we work together, the packs will be stronger." His scowl softened as he considered her words.

Then Silver Fire turned to the crowd and raised her voice. "I'm looking forward to working with you all!"

Summarize

Use important details from *The Wolves of Yellowstone* to summarize the story. Your graphic organizer may help.

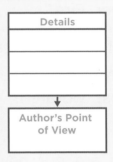

Text Evidence

1. How do you know that this story is a fantasy? **GENRE**

2. From what point of view is this story told? Give examples from the text that show the narrator's point of view. **POINT OF VIEW**

3. What does Silver Fire mean when she says she wants to "run for leader of the Wolf Council" on page 11? **IDIOMS**

4. Write about how this story would be different if it were told by a first-person narrator. **WRITE ABOUT READING**

Compare Texts

Read about why some people run for mayor.

Who Wants to Be Mayor?

Have you ever been a group leader or the captain of a sports team? The mayor of a local community is a leader, too.

Electing a Mayor

Many towns and cities in the United States have a local town or city council. The size of a council depends on the size of the town or city. The leaders of large cities, such as New York and Los Angeles, have a lot of responsibility.

A mayor usually leads a town or city council. It is the mayor's responsibility to manage the council in taking care of the interests and needs of the community.

Mayors are elected for a period of time, often for two to four years. There are rules about how many times a mayor can be reelected.

A Mayor's Responsibilities

A mayor has many responsibilities. He or she works with council members to plan how to use the money in the council's budget. The money is spent on community projects and services, such as libraries, parks, sports centers, and trash collection.

Mayors and their councils also make decisions about schools and housing. They consider ideas for bringing new jobs to the community. They make sure that local businesses follow health, safety, and environmental rules. Mayors and councils also work with the state government to meet the needs of local areas.

Mayors work in the Town Hall or council buildings.

The State Constitution

The United States is so big that each state has its own government. States also have state constitutions, which protect the rights of their citizens. The state government and town or city councils share responsibilities and work together to help things run smoothly in communities throughout the state.

Many mayors lead the council meetings. These meetings are held to discuss issues that affect the community. New laws are voted on at council meetings. Sometimes the mayor has the final vote when the council is making a difficult decision.

As a leader, the mayor attends and speaks at special ceremonies, parades, and festivals. If an important visitor, such as the state governor, comes to town, the mayor will often welcome them.

The job of mayor is perfect for people who like to lead and work for their local communities. Mayors know that local communities are better when people work, play, and enjoy their community together.

Mayors often attend ceremonies to open new businesses or buildings.

Make Connections

What does a mayor do? ESSENTIAL QUESTION

What connections can you make between Silver Fire's reasons for wanting to be a leader in *The Wolves of Yellowstone* and the responsibilities of a mayor in *Who Wants to Be Mayor*? TEXT TO TEXT

Focus on Literary Elements

Onomatopoeia Onomatopoeia means a word that sounds like the thing it represents. Animal Sounds are a good example of onomatopoeia. *Woof, meow, croak,* and *cluck* all sound like the sounds made by different animals.

Read and Find On page 2 in *The Wolves of Yellowstone*, the word *howl* invites you to draw out the long "ow" sound in the middle, just like the sound a howling wolf makes.

On the same page, the word *yipping* has a short, clipped quality to it, much like the high-pitched barks wolf pups make.

Your Turn

Write a soundscape using onomatopoeia. Make a T-chart with the heading "Setting" for one column and "Sounds" for the other. Fill in the chart with at least four settings and two or three sounds you would hear in each setting. Then write one sentence for each setting using the sounds from your chart. Read the lines out loud and make adjustments if needed. Illustrate your soundscape and share it with others.